5S Sustainment Schedule

Start Date: ____________________ Work Area: ____________________

Person Responsible	Specific Location	Frequency of Activity	Activities to Perform

A **Productivity Press** Product

www.enna.com
www.productivitypress.com

5S Sustainment Schedule

Start Date: ____________________ Work Area: ______________________

Person Responsible	Specific Location	Frequency of Activity	Activities to Perform

5S Sustainment Schedule

Start Date: ____________________ Work Area: ____________________

Person Responsible	Specific Location	Frequency of Activity	Activities to Perform

5S Sustainment Schedule

Start Date: ____________________ Work Area: ______________________

Person Responsible	Specific Location	Frequency of Activity	Activities to Perform

5S Sustainment Schedule

Start Date: ____________________ Work Area: ____________________

Person Responsible	Specific Location	Frequency of Activity	Activities to Perform

5S Sustainment Schedule

Start Date: ____________________ Work Area: ____________________

Person Responsible	Specific Location	Frequency of Activity	Activities to Perform

5S Sustainment Schedule

Start Date: ____________________ Work Area: ____________________

Person Responsible	Specific Location	Frequency of Activity	Activities to Perform

5S Sustainment Schedule

Start Date: ____________________ Work Area: ____________________

Person Responsible	Specific Location	Frequency of Activity	Activities to Perform

5S Sustainment Schedule

Start Date: ____________________ Work Area: ______________________

Person Responsible	Specific Location	Frequency of Activity	Activities to Perform

5S Sustainment Schedule

Start Date: ____________________ Work Area:____________________

Person Responsible	Specific Location	Frequency of Activity	Activities to Perform

5S Sustainment Schedule

Start Date: ____________________ Work Area: ____________________

Person Responsible	Specific Location	Frequency of Activity	Activities to Perform

5S Sustainment Schedule

Start Date: ____________________ Work Area: ______________________

Person Responsible	Specific Location	Frequency of Activity	Activities to Perform

5S Sustainment Schedule

Start Date: ____________________ Work Area: ____________________

Person Responsible	Specific Location	Frequency of Activity	Activities to Perform

5S Sustainment Schedule

Start Date: ____________________ Work Area: ____________________

Person Responsible	Specific Location	Frequency of Activity	Activities to Perform

5S Sustainment Schedule

Start Date: ____________________ Work Area: ____________________

Person Responsible	Specific Location	Frequency of Activity	Activities to Perform

5S Sustainment Schedule

Start Date: ____________________ Work Area: ____________________

Person Responsible	Specific Location	Frequency of Activity	Activities to Perform

5S Sustainment Schedule

Start Date: ____________________ Work Area: ____________________

Person Responsible	Specific Location	Frequency of Activity	Activities to Perform

5S Sustainment Schedule

Start Date: ____________________ Work Area: ____________________

Person Responsible	Specific Location	Frequency of Activity	Activities to Perform

5S Sustainment Schedule

Start Date: ____________________ Work Area: ____________________

Person Responsible	Specific Location	Frequency of Activity	Activities to Perform

5S Sustainment Schedule

Start Date: ____________________ Work Area: ____________________

Person Responsible	Specific Location	Frequency of Activity	Activities to Perform

5S Sustainment Schedule

Start Date: ____________________ Work Area: ____________________

Person Responsible	Specific Location	Frequency of Activity	Activities to Perform

5S Sustainment Schedule

Start Date: ____________________ Work Area: ____________________

Person Responsible	Specific Location	Frequency of Activity	Activities to Perform

5S Sustainment Schedule

Start Date: ____________________ Work Area: ____________________

Person Responsible	Specific Location	Frequency of Activity	Activities to Perform

5S Sustainment Schedule

Start Date: ____________________ Work Area: ______________________

Person Responsible	Specific Location	Frequency of Activity	Activities to Perform